THOMAS JEFFERSON AND THE GROWING UNITED STATES

(1800-1811)

TITLE LIST

THOMAS JEFFERSON AND THE GROWING UNITED STATES
(1800-1811)

BY CONSTANCE SHARP

MASON CREST

Mason Crest
370 Reed Road
Broomall, Pennsylvania 19008
www.masoncrest.com

Printed and bound in Hashemite Kingdom of Jordan.

First printing
9 8 7 6 5 4 3 2 1

Library of Congress Cataloging-in-Publication Data

Sharp, Constance.
  Thomas Jefferson and the growing United States (1800-1811) / by Constance Sharp.
      p. cm. — (How America became America)
  Includes bibliographical references and index.
  ISBN 978-1-4222-2400-7 (hardcover) — ISBN 978-1-4222-2396-3 (hardcover series) ISBN 978-1-4222-9310-2 (ebook)
  1. Jefferson, Thomas, 1743-1826—Juvenile literature. 2. Louisiana Purchase—Juvenile literature. 3. United States—Territorial expansion—History—19th century—Juvenile literature. I. Title.
  E332.79.S53 2012
  973.4'6092—dc22
  [B]
                              2011000692

Produced by Harding House Publishing Services, Inc.
www.hardinghousepages.com
Cover design by Torque Advertising + Design.

1603–James I becomes king.

1801–Thomas Jefferson is the first President to begin his work at the new capital, Washington, D.C.

1811–William Henry Harrison and his troops destroy the Shawnee camp on the Tippecanoe River. Harrison earns the nickname "Old Tippecanoe."

1803–Thomas Jefferson approves the Louisiana Purchase.

1811–President James Madison sends troops to Florida.

1754–The French and Indian War begins.

1810–People in Baton Rouge, Louisiana, make their own government as the Republic of West Florida.

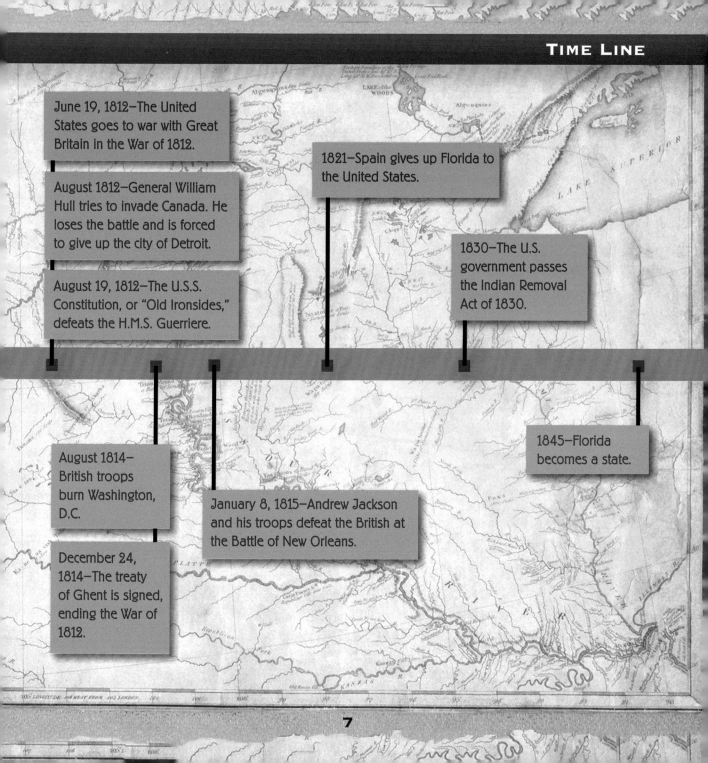

June 19, 1812–The United States goes to war with Great Britain in the War of 1812.

August 1812–General William Hull tries to invade Canada. He loses the battle and is forced to give up the city of Detroit.

August 19, 1812–The U.S.S. Constitution, or "Old Ironsides," defeats the H.M.S. Guerriere.

1821–Spain gives up Florida to the United States.

1830–The U.S. government passes the Indian Removal Act of 1830.

August 1814– British troops burn Washington, D.C.

December 24, 1814–The treaty of Ghent is signed, ending the War of 1812.

January 8, 1815–Andrew Jackson and his troops defeat the British at the Battle of New Orleans.

1845–Florida becomes a state.

Chapter One
JEFFERSON'S IDEAS ABOUT AMERICA

In 1776, Thomas Jefferson wrote the Declaration of Independence. The United States would be a new country. It would no longer be a part of Britain.

"All men are created equal," Jefferson wrote in the Declaration of Independence. He believed that everyone has certain rights. You didn't have to earn these rights. They belonged to you just because you were alive. The rights he was talking about were things like "life, **liberty**, and the **pursuit** of happiness."

Jefferson had strong beliefs. He put these beliefs into the Declaration of Independence. He wanted them to be a part of the United States right from the very beginning. He wanted the United States to be like no other country in the world.

A **declaration** is a statement. Often it's a piece of paper where people have written down the things they will stand up for.

Independence means being free to do what you want, without depending on anyone else to tell you what to do.

Liberty is another word for freedom.

Pursuit means going after something.

Jefferson was the country's first Secretary of State. He helped President George Washington run the new country.

Jefferson worried about the new country. He worried that some people wanted the United States to be a lot like Britain. He was afraid the government might start to act like a **monarchy**. He didn't want only the rich and powerful people to have the say in what happened in the United States. The United States was supposed to be a place where everyone was equal.

The country started dividing into two groups. One group, the Federalists, thought that the national government should be stronger than the states' government. They thought the federal (the national) government should be able to control what the state governments did. The other group was the Democratic-Republicans. They believed the state governments should have more power. They didn't want one government to run the country the way Britain had.

Thomas Jefferson was a Democratic-Republican. He believed very strongly that ordinary people made the United States great. Most of the Federalists disagreed. They thought ordinary people weren't smart

John Adams

A **monarchy** is a type of government where a king or a queen rules the country.

enough to govern themselves. They thought the rich and educated people should make decisions for the whole country. Jefferson wanted everyone, rich and poor, to get a good education. He thought everyone could learn to make good decisions.

Jefferson ran for president of the United States in 1796. John Adams, a Federalist, ran against him. John Adams became president, because he had the most votes. Jefferson got the second-highest number of votes, so he became vice-president.

While he was president, Adams approved new taxes. He also passed the Alien and **Sedition Acts**. The Alien and Sedition Acts made it harder to become a United States **citizen**. They also said the President could make foreigners leave if he thought they might be dangerous.

Jefferson didn't like the Alien and Sedition Acts. Most of the **immigrants** coming to the United States were poor. These immigrants were more likely to support

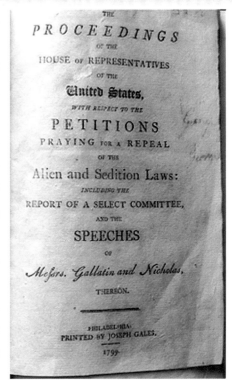

Many people disliked the Alien and Sedition Acts.

Sedition means getting people to go against the official government.

Acts are rules that have been made into law.

A **citizen** is a person who has full legal rights in the country he lives in.

Immigrants are people who have moved from their country to make a new home in another country.

A small, family farm.

the Democrat-Republicans. If they couldn't become citizens, they wouldn't be able to vote, though.

Other people were upset about the Alien and Sedition Acts, too. They didn't like how Adams and the Federalists were trying to take all the power. In 1800, at the next presidential election, the Democrat-Republicans won. This time, Jefferson became president. The first thing Jefferson did as president was to get rid of the Alien and Sedition Acts. He wanted to be fair to everyone.

Three main things were important to Jefferson. These were independence, religious freedom, and education. To Jefferson, independence meant more than having a say in government. It also meant being able to take care of your own needs. It meant having enough money to live comfortably.

Jefferson thought the United States should be a country of little family farms. Everyone would be able to grow the food they needed. They would be able to make or grow the things they needed to live. He thought working on farms would be good for people, too.

A lot of people didn't like Jefferson's idea. They wanted to be rich—but small family farms didn't make much money. Instead, they just made enough for people to live. Big plantations could make more money.

Big plantations needed slaves to work the land. Jefferson thought slavery was evil. He thought it was terrible thing, but he didn't know how to end it. He thought maybe the slaves should be freed a little at a time. He was afraid that freeing them all at once would be too hard on the country. He thought people who owned slaves needed to find other ways to do the work. He was afraid that if the slaves were freed, they would turn on the white people and fight them.

Jefferson wasn't sure how to make many of his ideas work. Still, Jefferson kept his beliefs.

Jefferson's home, Monticello

Chapter Two
JEFFERSON'S REAL STORY

Thomas Jefferson had good ideas. But those ideas weren't the whole story. Thomas Jefferson's real story didn't always match up with his ideas.

Jefferson thought everyone should be free. But he didn't know how to end slavery. He thought everyone should work hard on a small family farm. But he also thought everyone should be educated. (And if you had to spend most of your time doing chores on your family's farm, it was hard to go to school!) He thought everyone should take part in the government. People who spent all their time working on a farm didn't have much time for government, either.

And Jefferson didn't live his own life in line with his beliefs. He didn't live on a small farm. Instead, he owned a huge plantation. He didn't believe in slavery. But he owned slaves who worked on his plantation.

Jefferson's home was called Monticello. It was a beautiful house. Jefferson had designed it himself. The house stood on five thousand acres of land. Jefferson loved Monticello. He spent a lot of money on it. When he was at home, he spent most of his days riding around the plantation on horseback. He loved taking care of Monticello. But it was too big for one man to farm, or even one man and his family. Nearly 150 slaves worked at Monticello.

Some people think Jefferson was a **hypocrite**. Jefferson had excuses for being the way he was. He just wasn't strong enough to change the way he lived.

Jefferson had been born into a slave-owning family. The only way of life he had ever known depended on slaves. Freeing the slaves meant changing his life completely. But the situation was even more complicated than that.

Slave cabins

Thomas Jefferson also owed a lot of money. Jefferson liked living a rich life. He had spent money he didn't actually have. Most of the money had gone to Monticello. Some had been used to buy expensive food and wine. Because he had so many debts, he couldn't free his slaves. Everything he owned—including the slaves— were **collateral** for his debts. That meant that the people he owed money to could take the slaves if Jefferson didn't pay his debt.

Jefferson worried about slavery a lot. He knew it was evil, but he don't know what to do. The best idea he could come up with was to end slavery gradually. He

A **hypocrite** is someone who says one thing and acts another way.

Collateral is something a person owns that is worth the amount of money he is borrowing. Having collateral shows he can pay the money back.

Native means people who have lived in a place for a very long time.

wanted to give the freed slaves a good education. He wanted them to be able to live good lives as independent people. He thought black people could be given a colony in Africa. He was afraid blacks and whites might have trouble living together.

Jefferson also dreamed that **Native** tribes would become part of America. He really liked Native cultures. He thought the Native people would make the United States stronger and better. He believed Natives and whites should have all the same rights.

But there was a big gap between Jefferson's dreams and the real story. A lot of people who study Jefferson's life don't think he tried very hard to make his dreams turn into reality. They say he missed a lot of chances to do the right thing. Slavery didn't end while he was president. And Native people didn't get the same rights as white people. Instead, they lost even more of their land.

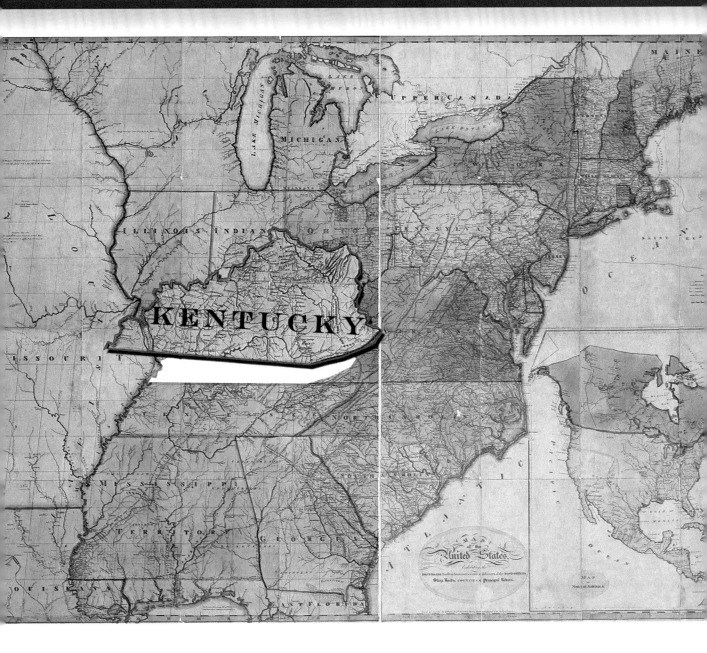

In 1792, Kentucky became a new state. People argued a lot about whether Kentucky would be a slave state (a state where slavery was allowed) or a free state (a state where slavery was against the law). People liked Jefferson. They respected him and his opinions. If he had tried, he might have been able to convince people to make Kentucky a free state. Jefferson didn't try to argue that Kentucky should be a free state, though.

So why didn't Jefferson stand up for his beliefs more? He probably had a lot of reasons.

Some historians think Jefferson wanted all the other plantation owners to like him. These men were his friends. He went to parties with them. They were the people he knew best. It would have been hard for him to go against all his friends.

Jefferson also really hated cities. He thought they were ugly and unhealthy. Cities, though, offered poor people the chance to get jobs in factories. Jefferson thought plantations were a better idea than factories. He didn't want people building cities in the new Western territories. He thought it would terrible to see the beautiful land covered with ugly cities. Instead, he wanted farmers to settle the West. He let slave owners move into the West to build plantations. For Jefferson, cities were even worse than slavery.

The real story never matched up with Jefferson's good ideas. He knew slavery would have to end. He hoped it would end soon. But he didn't do anything to make it happen. It would take the Civil War before that would happen.

In the meantime, Jefferson did help build the United States in other ways. One of the most important things he did was make the United States bigger than it had ever been before.

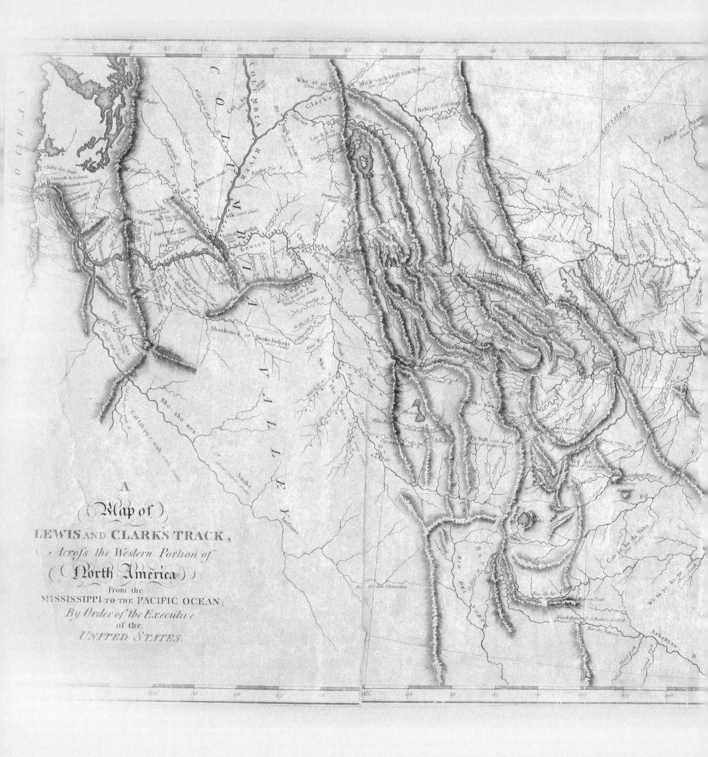

A
Map of
LEWIS AND CLARK'S TRACK,
Across the Western Portion of
North America
From the
MISSISSIPPI TO THE PACIFIC OCEAN;
By Order of the Executive
of the
UNITED STATES.

Chapter Three
THE LOUISIANA PURCHASE

When people talked about Louisiana in 1800, they didn't mean the same thing they mean today. Today, Louisiana is a Southern state on the Gulf of Mexico. In 1800, Louisiana was a huge piece of land. It stretched from the Gulf of Mexico north to the Great Lakes. It went all the way from the Appalachian Mountains west to the Rocky Mountains.

Most of the people who lived in Louisiana at that time were Natives. They belonged to tribes who had lived there for thousands of years. Despite this, France had claimed the area in 1682. Some French people settled there, mostly in the area around New Orleans.

Over the next hundred years, the land passed back and forth between Spain and France. Then, when Napoleon ruled France, he decided he wanted to rule the entire world. He thought taking control of Louisiana once and for all would help him. So he sent soldiers to get the job done. On the way to Louisiana, though, he told his soldiers to stop by the island of St. Domingue.

St. Domingue was a French colony in the Caribbean Sea. Ten years earlier, the slaves there had rebelled. They were very brave, and they had made up their minds to be free. And they won! They began ruling themselves.

Napoleon didn't think it would take much to get the colony back under French control. He thought it would be a little job his soldiers could do on their way to Louisiana.

The people of St. Domingue were not going to give up so easily. The French soldiers stayed for seven months. Most of them died. Finally, Napoleon gave up on the colony. He was spending too much money on it. And he was getting nowhere. In 1804, St. Domingue became the independent country of Haiti.

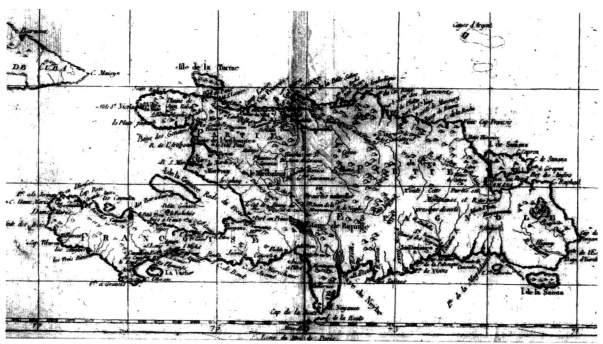

Map of St. Domingue

All this trouble made Napoleon worry about Louisiana. He couldn't afford to spend a lot of money on this colony, too.

Meanwhile, when Thomas Jefferson was president, he heard rumors that France would be taking over Louisiana. He didn't like the idea of France owning part of North America. He was afraid Napoleon would try to take over the United States next. So Jefferson sent a man named Robert Livingston to France. Livingston's job was to convince France not to move into Louisiana.

Livingston was frustrated with his job. He wasn't sure how he was going to do it. Nobody except Napoleon had any power in France—and Napoleon wouldn't talk to him. Livingston wasn't even sure if France or Spain owned Louisiana.

In 1803, Jefferson sent James Monroe to France to help Livingston. Monroe would offer to buy part of Louisiana from the French. Jefferson hoped to be able to buy New Orleans and the land east of the city. If Napoleon refused to sell, Monroe and Livingston would go next to Britain. There, they would try to make an agreement with the British. If the United States had to go to war with France, Jefferson wanted Britain to help America.

(top) James Monroe, (bottom) Robert Livingston

Charles-Maurice de Talleyrand

The day before Monroe got to France, though, Livingston had a surprise. Talleyrand, the French foreign minister, asked to meet with him. And then Talleyrand suddenly asked Livingston how much the United States would pay for all Louisiana.

The next day, when Monroe got there, Livingston talked to him about the offer. They didn't know what to do. Jefferson had told Monroe to buy a much smaller piece of land, not the whole Louisiana Territory! Monroe and Livingston couldn't ask Jefferson what he wanted to do. They didn't have telephones or the Internet! Letters took months to travel back and forth across the Atlantic Ocean by boat.

Finally, Monroe and Livingston decided to make the purchase. The price they finally agreed on with Napoleon was 15 million dollars. They also agreed to let France use the ports in Louisiana for free.

The port of New Orleans

"LET THE LAND REJOICE FOR YOU HAVE BOUGHT LOUISIANA FOR A SONG"
GEN. HORATIO GATES TO JEFFERSON ON JULY 18, 1803

"Let the land rejoice for you have bought Louisiana for a song"
(inscription on a gunstock given to Jefferson)

Monroe and Livingston had to borrow the 15 million dollars. Britain was happy to lend them the money. Britain didn't want France to have too much power. The British government was glad France wouldn't be taking over Louisiana after all.

Monroe and Livingston were nervous about what Jefferson would say. When Jefferson got the news about the Louisiana Purchase, though, he was thrilled. It was more than he had hoped for. He was glad to have more land for the United States. He had dreamed that the country could expand westward. Now it could.

Congress agreed with Jefferson. On December 20, 1803, the United States took control of the entire Louisiana Territory. It was 820,000 square miles of land! Now the United States owned the entire middle section of North America.

Chapter Four
LEWIS AND CLARK

Thomas Jefferson was delighted that at least one of his dreams for America had come true. Now he wanted to find out more about the new land.

In the early 1800s, Americans didn't know very much about the land that lay to the west. The Spanish had settled the West Coast. A lot of the land between the oceans was a mystery, though.

In 1803, President Thomas Jefferson had an idea. He decided the United States would explore the continent to the west. Meriwether Lewis, Jefferson's secretary, would lead the **expedition**. William Clark, Lewis's friend, would be the other leader. Lewis and Clark, with a group of other men, would look for a good water route across the continent. A trade route across the country would be good for the United States. It would mean the country could do business with people on the West Coast.

The United States didn't own all the land Lewis and Clark would be traveling across. The Spanish owned part of it. The British owned part, too. Jefferson didn't want these countries to know the United States was thinking of expanding. The expedition would have to be a secret.

An **expedition** is a trip taken to explore a new place.

Lewis and Clark explored the rivers that ran into the Mississippi.

A drawing of one of the wildlife specimens brought back by Lewis and Clark

Drawn for Capt. M. Lewis (1806?) by C.W. Peale

Jefferson wanted to know all about the land to the west. He wanted to know what the land was like. He wanted to know what the weather was like. He wanted to know all about the people who lived there. Besides looking for a good trade route, Lewis and Clark would gather information. They would learn about the Native tribes they met. They would collect plants. They would study the animals they saw. They would write down everything they saw and did.

The Flatheads were one of the tribes Lewis and Clark encountered.

Jefferson gave Lewis a lot of instructions for the journey. He wanted the expedition to make friends with the Native tribes they met. They were to tell them that the United States wanted to live peacefully with them. Jefferson wanted to do what he could to make friends with the Western tribes.

The Lewis and Clark expedition left from a camp near St. Louis in the spring of 1804. They crossed the Mississippi River and entered the mouth of the Missouri River. For the next year and a half, they traveled west. They weren't able to find the easy water route they had hoped to find. They learned a lot, though. They made maps. They brought back descriptions of 122 new animals and 178 new plants. They learned about the Native tribes they met. They brought back descriptions of their culture and languages.

Statue of Sacajawea

Lewis and Clark needed a guide on their voyage. They hired a French fur trader named Toussaint Charbonneau. Charbonneau brought along his wife, a Native woman named Sacajawea. She spoke some of the Native languages, so he brought her along.

Sacajawea was only seventeen years old when she and her husband joined the group. She had a baby boy named Jean Baptiste. The other members of the expedition loved the little boy. They nicknamed him "Pompy."

Most of the men on the expedition didn't like Sacajawea's husband, though. They were upset with him for hitting Sacajawea. They were also annoyed with him when he panicked during a storm and nearly tipped over a boat.

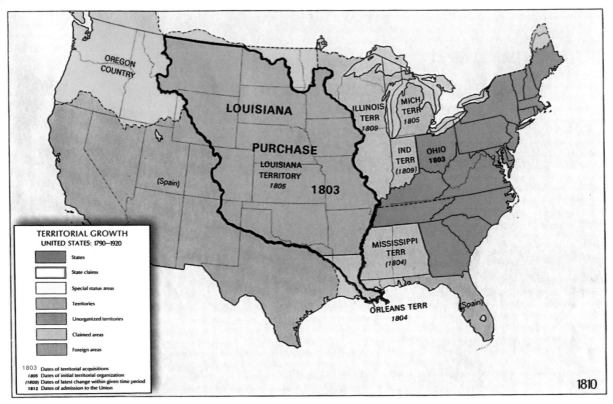

Map showing growth of the United States.

Lewis and Clark hadn't thought much about Sacajawea at first. She was a woman and she was a Native. Most European men at that time thought both those things meant Sacajawea was worth less. They didn't expect her to be as smart as a white man. They didn't think she would be able to do much. Especially since she had a baby with her.

Instead, Sacajawea turned out to be very helpful. She knew the area. This meant she could help Lewis and Clark decide where to go. She knew the kinds of things that were good to eat. She could help them talk to the Native tribes they met. The Native

Example of a covered wagon used by settlers moving west.

people they met trusted them because they traveled with a woman and a child. If they had come to attack and fight, people thought, they would have left her behind.

Even though Lewis and Clark didn't find a simple trade route across North America, their expedition changed the United States. The information the group brought back got people interested in the West. More and more people started moving west. The United States was expanding.

Settlers moving west brought up more questions, though. What about slavery? Should people be able to bring slaves west? Would slavery be allowed in the new Louisiana Territory?

Congress argued a lot about these questions. Many Southern congressmen said people wouldn't be able to farm or make money without slavery. They said white men couldn't survive in the heat of the Southwestern climate. They said slaves were the only people who could work in the heat. Slave owners moving west brought their slaves with them. Slavery continued to spread across the southwestern United States.

Again, Jefferson didn't do anything to stop slavery from spreading. He was more worried about other problems American was facing.

Slaves working with cotton gin

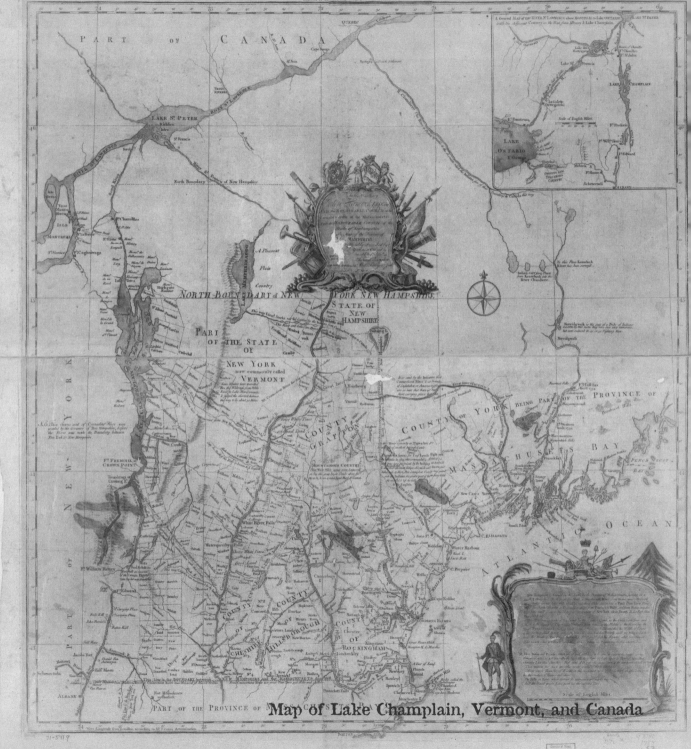

Map of Lake Champlain, Vermont, and Canada

Chapter Five
AMERICA STAYS OUT OF EUROPE'S WARS

The countries of Europe had been fighting with each other for a long time. Each country wanted to be the strongest. But the United States didn't want to get caught in Europe's wars. It was a young country. Thomas Jefferson and the other leaders wanted to focus on building up the United States. They had enough problems at home without getting mixed up with Europe's problems.

Britain and France were in the middle of a war. They were both powerful countries. They were strong in different ways, though. France had a stronger army. Britain had a stronger navy. And both sides wanted to use the United States to help them win the war.

To try to make their navy stronger, France started capturing American ships. Whenever American merchants sailed to Britain to buy and sell goods, they risked being captured. The French would then use the American ships in their fight against Britain.

The British didn't make things easy for the United States, either. The British navy started something called impressment. This meant it would capture men and force them to serve in the British navy. "Press gangs" would walk around cities, looking for sailors.

When they found one, they would kidnap him and "press" him into service. Press gangs worked at sea, too. When they came across an American ship, they would board it. They would look for men they could take for their navy. They ignored the fact that most of these men were American citizens. During this time, press gangs took about six thousand men from American ships.

The people of the United States were very angry about impressment. They were angry about how the French captured their ships, too. Some people wanted the United States to go to war against both Britain and France.

The press gang

A battle at sea

President Thomas Jefferson didn't want to go to war. He knew the United States couldn't handle a war. For one thing, America had a very small army. Jefferson didn't like strong armies. He believed they could be used to control the people in their own country. After all, this was what was happening in Napoleon's France.

Jefferson wanted the United States to stay out of the war. He knew something had to be done, though. Instead of war, he suggested a **trade embargo**.

A **trade embargo** is when one country stops doing business with another country.

This "O-Grab-Me" cartoon (embargo spelled backwards) shows how unpopular the Embargo Act was with Americans.

The United States sold cotton, tobacco, and grain to Europe. An embargo would mean that the United States wouldn't trade these things anymore. Jefferson hoped this would show France and Britain how much they needed the United States' goods. Congress agreed with Jefferson. In 1807, it passed the Embargo Act.

The Act didn't work out like Jefferson had hoped, though. Europe had lots of American goods piled in warehouses. They wouldn't start running out for several years.

Jefferson had wanted the Embargo Act to hurt Europe. Instead, it ended up hurting the United States. People who made their living shipping goods to and from Europe suddenly didn't have a job. In the South, plantation owners lost their biggest buyers. In the North, people relied on goods from Europe. Factories no longer had the parts they needed. Many of them went out of business.

Something that is **smuggled** is brought into a country illegally.

Smugglers unloading their goods

People were very upset about the Embargo Act. This was not what they had wanted the government to do to solve their problems with Europe. In the North, along the border with Canada, people ignored the embargo. They **smuggled** goods back and forth across the border.

Political cartoon depicting the "death" of the Embargo Act.

Jefferson had always worried that the army could be used against its own people. Now, he found himself sending in the army to control the smuggling. The army patrolled the Canadian border. Usually, the smugglers managed to get through anyway.

The Embargo Act wasn't working. It wasn't doing what Jefferson had wanted it to do. In 1809, three days before Jefferson stopped being president, he ended the Act. Now the United States could trade with all European countries except France and Britain. The next year, President James Madison cancelled this part of the Act too.

One good thing did happen because of the Embargo Act. Since they couldn't get things they needed from Europe, the United States had to find ways to manage. More factories started opening up to make the goods the country needed. While the Embargo Act was in effect, the industries in the United States got stronger.

During Thomas Jefferson's time as president, the United States changed a lot. The Louisiana Purchase doubled the size of the country. The Lewis and Clark expedition had mapped the West.

Jefferson was very important to the beginnings of the United States. Today, a lot of people still respect him. Our leaders still quote him.

Thomas Jefferson
A Philosopher a Patriote and a Friend

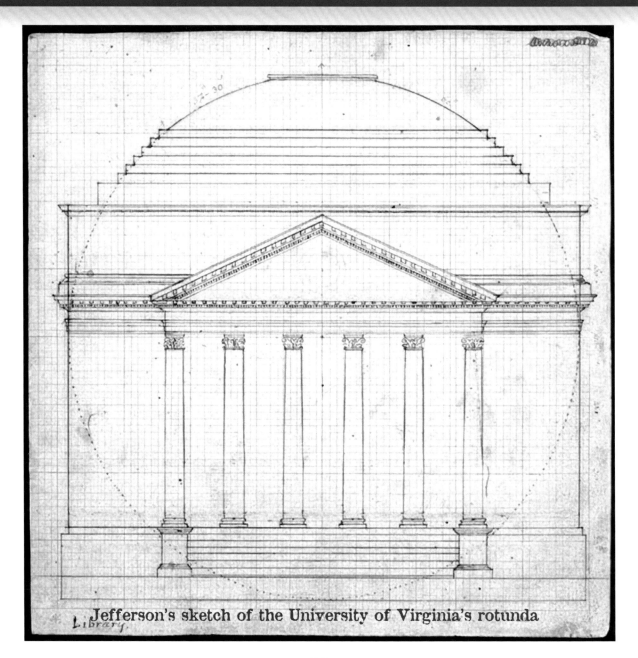

Jefferson's sketch of the University of Virginia's rotunda

But some people wonder if the United States should stop honoring him. After all, he owned slaves and didn't do much to end slavery—even though he said he hated slavery. He opened up the West for settlement, driving thousands of Native people from their homes—even though he claimed to love and respect Native culture.

Jefferson said one thing and did another. He could have done more to build a better country. But he did do important things that were good.

He built the University of Virginia. The university took students who wanted to learn. They didn't have to have money to pay for their education. The university was one of the things Jefferson was most proud of at the end of his life.

The original plan for the University of Virginia

Another thing Jefferson was very proud of was the Virginia Act for Establishing Religious Freedom. This act said all people could have their own religious ideas. It said nobody could be forced to go to a certain church or give money to a certain church. He believed that the church and the government should be kept separate. This idea is still very important to Americans.

Jefferson had great ideas for the United States. Sometimes, he didn't know how to make his ideas work. Still, he started Americans thinking about a lot of the freedoms we still have in the twenty-first century. He helped shape the country where we live today.

Thomas Jefferson, third President of the United States (1801–1809)

FIND OUT MORE

In Books

Bruchac, Joseph. *Sacajawea*. Boston, Mass.: Houghton Mifflin Harcourt Publishing, 2008.

Burgan, Michael. *The Louisiana Purchase.* Chicago, Ill.: Heinemann Library, 2007.

Doeden, Matt. *Thomas Jefferson: Great American*. Mankato, Minn.: Capstone Press, 2006.

Elston, Heidi. *Thomas Jefferson*. Edina, Minn.: ABDO Publishing Company, 2009.

Herbert, Janis. *Lewis and Clark for Kids*. Chicago, Ill.: Chicago Review Press, 2000.

Isaacs, Sally. *Life on a Southern Plantation*. Chicago, Ill.: Reed Educational & Professional Publishing, 2000.

Ransom, Candice. *Lewis and Clark*. Minneapolis, Minn.: Lerner Publications, 2003.

On the Internet

Jefferson and Slavery
classroom.monticello.org/kids/resources/profile/263/Jefferson-and-Slavery/

The Lewis and Clark Trail
www.lewisandclarktrail.com/101.htm

The Lewis and Clark Trail (photographs)
www.lewisandclarkpictures.com

The Louisiana Purchase
www.socialstudiesforkids.com/articles/ushistory/louisianapurchase.htm

Monticello (Jefferson's Home)
www.monticello.org/

Napoleon's Empire
www.kidspast.com/world-history/0390-napoleons-empire.php

Sacagawea
www.mce.k12tn.net/indians/famous/sacajawea.htm

Thomas Jefferson Quotes
www.brainyquote.com/quotes/authors/t/thomas_jefferson.html

Thomas Jefferson
www.socialstudiesforkids.com/subjects/thomasjefferson.htm

INDEX

ABOUT THE AUTHOR
AND THE CONSULTANT

Constance Sharp studied history and literature in college. She enjoys teaching children about the history of their world.

Dr. Jack N. Rakove is a professor of history and American studies at Stanford University, where he is director of American studies. The winner of the 1997 Pulitzer Prize in history, Dr. Rakove is the author of *The Unfinished Election of 2000*, *Constitutional Culture and Democratic Rule*, and *James Madison and the Creation of the American Republic*. He is also the president of the Society for the History of the Early American Republic.